SKYSURFING

HOLLY CEFREY

HIGH
interest
books

Children's Press®
A Division of Scholastic Inc.
New York / Toronto / London / Auckland / Sydney
Mexico City / New Delhi / Hong Kong
Danbury, Connecticut

Book Design: Michael DeLisio
Contributing Editor: Jennifer Silate
Photo Credits: Cover © Zefa Visual Media-Germany/Index Stock Imagery, Inc.;
back cover © Duomo/Corbis; title page, p. 3 © Photogear; pp. 5, 23 © Steve
Fitchett/Getty Images; pp. 6, 13, 32 © Joe McBride/Getty Images; pp. 8, 11, 18,
34 © Brian Erler/Getty Images; pp. 15, 28, 30 © Jump Run Productions/Getty
Images; p. 16 © Joe McBride/Corbis; p. 20 © Aerial Focus/Index Stock Imagery,
Inc.; p. 24 © Bettmann/Corbis; p. 27 © ASAP Ltd./Index Stock Imagery, Inc.;
p. 36 © Jussi Laine/Getty Images

Library of Congress Cataloging-in-Publication Data

Cefrey, Holly.
    Skysurfing / Holly Cefrey.
    v. cm. – (X-treme outdoors)
    Includes bibliographical references and index.
    Contents: Skysurfing 101 – Surf events and champions – Surfing the
    skies – Getting airborne.
    ISBN 0-516-24318-7 (lib. bdg.) – ISBN 0-516-24380-2 (pbk.)
    1. Skysurfing–Juvenile literature. [1. Skysurfing. 2. Skydiving.] I.
    Title: Sky surfing. II. Title. III. Series.

    GV770.23 .C44 2003
    797.5'6–dc21
                                        2002007941

CONTENTS

INTRODUCTION

Your plane is soaring 13,000 feet (3,962 meters) above the ground. Looking out, all you see is blue sky. The moment you've waited for has finally come: It's time to dive. You jump out of the plane and begin free-falling. The wind screams in your ears. You spin, flip, and twist in the air with your skyboard attached to your feet. Your heart is pumping as you plummet to Earth at about 120 miles (193 kilometers) per hour. Your partner flies around you, trying to capture each of your movements with a video recorder. In 60 seconds, you have fallen almost 10,000 feet (3,048 m). It's time to open your parachute. You release your parachute from the pack on your back. Your free fall is over. With the canopy of your chute open, you sail safely down to the ground. Skysurfing is such a thrill, you can't wait to do it again!

Falling or flying? Skysurfers take sporting to the extreme.

Extreme heights and speeds make skysurfing one of the most thrilling sports in the world. Skysurfers must balance themselves on a skyboard while falling more than 160 feet (49 m) per second. Special equipment and skills, along with physical strength, are needed to become a skysurfer. Read on to find out more about one of the world's most *X-treme* sports.

CHAPTER ONE

SKYSURFING 101

The sport of skysurfing began with skydiving. Skydiving is the sport of jumping from an airplane and free-falling before opening a parachute. A skydiver jumps out of a plane, free-falls toward Earth, then opens his or her parachute. Not long ago, some skydivers began to experiment during free fall. This led to the creation of new sky sports, such as freestyle and skysurfing. These new sports are also known as alternative flying.

ALTERNATIVE FLYING

Freestyle is a sport in which a skydiver performs acrobatic moves during free fall. It is a team sport. Freestyle teams have at least two members. One

What's more fun than jumping from an airplane with a skyboard strapped to your feet? Nothing — if you're a skysurfer.

The cameraflyer and skysurfer are a match made in heaven.

member, the cameraflyer, videotapes his or her partner's moves. The cameraflyer must move around, above, and under the performer in order to get the most exciting video footage possible. During competition, the score that a freestyle team receives is based on both acrobatic moves and camera work.

X-FACTOR

The first successful parachute jump from an airplane was made in 1912.

Skysurfing is also a team sport. A skysurfing team is made up of a skysurfer and a cameraflyer. Like a freestyler, the skysurfer also performs acrobatic moves during free fall. However, the skysurfer performs the moves with a skyboard strapped to his or her feet. The skysurfer must stay balanced and in control while performing on the board. This is easier said than done. Many skydiving schools and instructors suggest that a student learn to master basic freestyle moves before even trying to skysurf.

LOFTY BEGINNINGS

In the 1980s, skydivers in the United States started to jump with boogie boards, which are short, fat boards that are used to surf ocean waves. The skydivers laid flat on the boards during free fall. This was called air surfing.

The first standing skysurf was performed by French skydiver Joël Cruciani. In 1987, he used a

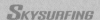

regular surfboard with snowboard-type foot bindings attached to it. Soon, other skydivers also started experimenting with skysurfing.

SKYSURFING FIRSTS

1990
- Pete McKeeman, a skydiver and cameraflyer, comes up with the idea to create teams with a cameraflyer and a freestyle performer for alternative flying competitions.
- Jerry Loftis is the first American to skysurf.

1992
- Jerry Loftis forms Surflite, the first company dedicated to making skyboards.

1994
- American Amy Baylie-Haass is the first female skysurfer to be shown in action on a television commercial for the Sony Handycam.

THE COMPETITIVE EDGE

Skydiving organizations played a major role in making skysurfing a worldwide sport. In 1992, the French organization for parachuting sports, the Fédération

Many people have flipped head over heels for skysurfing.

Français de Parachutisme (FFP), recognized skysurfing as an official sport. The FFP established guidelines for manufacturers of skysurfing equipment. It also started programs for skysurfing training. Soon, other organizations began to recognize the sport. Each created its own guidelines and skysurfing events.

The World Freestyle Federation (WFF) held competitive freestyle skydiving events. In 1993, the American-based WFF created the first set of rules for competitive skysurfing. These rules were accepted and used by several skysurfing competitions throughout the United States and Europe. Skysurfing was also included in the 1993 WFF World Championships, held in Spain. Patrick de Gayardon and Gus Wing became the first world champion skysurfing team. The following year, Gaudenzia Martinengo and Jerôme Erlich became the first women skysurf world champions. The WFF ended in 1995. Fortunately, other organizations, such as Skysports International (SSI), continued to support skysurfing and other sky sports.

Rules and guidelines of a skysurfing competition depend upon the organization that holds the event. Each organization has its own competition rules. Some organizations consulted with expert skysurfers,

In competitions, skysurfers begin their performance as soon as they leave the plane.

such as Patrick de Gayardon, while forming rules or guidelines. Many organizations' members are skydivers or skysurfers.

Skysurfing was featured on television in the 1995 ESPN Extreme Games (now the ESPN X Games). People around the world finally got a glimpse of this exciting new sport. In 1996, SSI announced the beginning of the first professional skysurfing tour, called the SSI Pro Tour. Skysurfers competed in four tour events to qualify for the 1996 ESPN X Games. The SSI Pro Tour events were held in Florida, Spain, Switzerland, and California.

COMPETITIVE EDGE

1990
- The first World Freestyle Championships are held.

1991
- The ESPN network airs part of the second World Freestyle Championships.

1993
- The first Skysurfing World Championships are held as a part of the fourth WFF World Championships in Spain.
- The WFF rules for skysurfing are used in skysurf competitions in California, Illinois, and France.

1994
- The women's division is added to the second annual Skysurfing World Championships for the first time.
- The world's first cash prize for skysurfing is awarded to first-place finishers.

1995
- The ESPN X Games include skysurfing as part of the competition. Skysurfers Rob Harris and Joe Jennings win $5,000.
- Skysports International (SSI) is formed.

1996
- The International Parachuting Commission (IPC) organizes the first World Cup of Freestyle Skydiving & Skysurfing.

Many women have become world-class skysurfers.

CHAPTER TWO

SURF EVENTS AND CHAMPIONS

Today, many skydive centers hold skysurf competitions. Alternative flying events and tours take place around the world. Competitions include the U.S. National Championships, hosted by Skydive Arizona and the SkyEuroCup, which is a European sky-sport tour. The winners of the SkyEuroCup are the European champions of their sky sport.

WE ARE THE CHAMPIONS

Skysurfing is a new sport, but there are already experts, champions, and legends. There aren't very many professional skysurfers, so many of the competitors work together and become friends.

Many skysurfers must perform hundreds of jumps before they are ready to compete.

A CAMERA IN THE SKY

Joe Jennings is a world-champion cameraflyer. He and Rob Harris, another skysurfing legend, were the first skysurfing team to win at the first ESPN X Games in 1995. Jennings has created Emmy Award-winning films and many popular commercials. Jennings has also shot stunts for the movies *Air Force One* and *Charlie's Angels*. He even videotaped a skydive that President George Bush made in 1997.

"It's a wonderful sport. Unfortunately, you have to be eighteen to start skydiving, so skysurfing is off-limits

Professional cameraflyers may work with freestyle teams and skysurfers.

to most youth," Jennings says. "I specialize in filming sky-surfers, and it's by far my favorite aerial subject.…Flying camera for skysurfers is a challenge. It's a bit like a fight-er pilot keeping another plane in his or her sights."

DYNAMIC DUO

Tanya Garcia-O'Brien and Craig O'Brien are a world-champion skysurfing team. O'Brien is the cameraflyer. Tanya is the skysurfer. This married couple has won two world championships and two U.S. National Championships. Tanya has also worked as a stunt dou-ble in movies such as *Charlie's Angels*. Craig and Tanya teach at the Perris Valley Skysurf School, in California.

THE BIRDMAN OF THE 21ST CENTURY

Patrick de Gayardon was admired by hundreds of fans and fellow skydivers. In eighteen years, he had com-pleted over 11,000 jumps. Gayardon helped to get skysurfing recognized as a sport. He also performed some of the most amazing skydiving moves. Once, Gayardon jumped *into* a flying plane. He was the first world champion of skysurfing. Unfortunately, in 1998, Gayardon died while skydiving in Hawaii.

CHAPTER THREE

GEARING UP FOR THE SURF

Experienced skysurfers know the importance of using the right equipment. Without the proper equipment, a skysurf can turn into a deadly event. Skysurfing equipment includes: a skyboard, special clothing, a video-mounted helmet, special instruments, and a rig. Equipment for one year can cost a team more than $14,000.

SKYBOARD

Skyboards cost around $700. Most skyboards are made of aluminum and graphite. Others are made of foam wrapped with fiberglass. Foot bindings are attached to the board. The bindings are part of a

Using proper technique and the right gear guarantees skysurfers a smooth-sailing experience.

release system, which allows the skysurfer to release the board from his or her feet by pulling a handle. The handle is attached to the waist of the skysurfer.

Skyboards weighing more than 0.7 grams per square centimeter have their own miniature parachute. If the skysurfer experiences an emergency, he or she can cut away, or drop the board, which will slowly return to the ground by itself.

CLOTHING

Skysurfers usually wear tight-fitting bottoms, such as Lycra sport tights. Tight clothing allows jumpers to move through the air easier than loose clothing. However, tops are usually loose. This is to balance the upper body of a skysurfer with the lower body, which has the skyboard attached. High-top shoes are recommended for ankle support.

Cameraflyers usually wear suits with wings attached from the wrists to the waist or the hips. The wings allow the cameraflyer to change his or her falling speed to match the speed of the skysurfer. When the wings are open, the cameraflyer falls less quickly.

In addition to wearing a loose top, leaning forward also helps skydivers keep their balance.

VIDEO-MOUNTED HELMET

Most cameraflyers use a digital camcorder that is attached to their helmet. A camcorder costs between $2,200 and $4,500. The helmet costs from $300 to $700. The helmet that the cameraflyer wears is specially designed to hold the camcorder. This leaves the cameraflyer's arms free to perform moves. More than one camcorder can be mounted on a helmet. During some competitions, helmets are equipped with transmitters. This allows the dive to be broadcast on television as it is being filmed.

SPECIAL INSTRUMENTS

Professional skysurfing teams are required to use altimeters. An altimeter measures the altitude of the skydiver. Altitude is the height of something above the ground. Altimeters are also used in airplanes to help pilots determine how high their planes are flying. Most skydivers wear altimeters on their wrist or chest. Some altimeters beep in the skydiver's ear when a preset altitude is reached. Altimeters are used by skydivers to determine the altitude at which they have to

Video-mounted helmets can weigh up to 10 pounds. If cameraflyers aren't careful, those 10 pounds can give them a big pain in the neck!

open their canopy in order to land safely. The canopy is the part of the parachute that catches the air. Some altimeters also record details such as the number of jumps and the average speed of the free fall. Altimeters cost from $100 to $400.

The teams are also required to use an AAD. An AAD is an automatic activation device. Sometimes, a skysurfer may be knocked unconscious during a fall. If that happens, the jumper would be unable to open his or her parachute. An AAD will open a reserve, or back-up parachute, if the skysurfer has not yet opened his or her canopy after passing a preset altitude. A good AAD costs about $1,200.

RIG

The rig consists of the harness, the container, a main parachute, a reserve parachute, and the AAD. The container holds the parachutes. It is attached to the diver's body by the harness.

A parachute slows an object as it falls to Earth by catching air. The main canopy and the reserve canopy in the rig are usually made of nylon. The diver opens the main canopy when he or she is about 3,000 to

A reserve canopy can save your life. It can cost between $50 to $75 for a professional to repack a reserve canopy.

2,000 feet (914 to 609 m) above the ground. Main canopies are reusable and get repacked by the diver after each use.

The most common canopy is rectangular shaped. The rectangular shape makes the canopy act like a wing. Rectangular-shaped canopies are much easier to steer and land than circular canopies. Early para-chutists, such as those in the armed forces, used circular canopies. The reserve canopy is opened only in emergencies. Once opened, reserve canopies can

A well-maintained rig will give you the confidence to surf the skies without a care in the world.

only be repacked by experts called riggers. For safety, the reserve canopy must be inspected every 120 days—even if it was never used. A full rig costs between $4,000 and $5,000.

SKYSURFING LINGO

Skysurfers have their own special language that they use when talking about their sport. Here are just a few of the terms:

Biff: when a diver misjudges his or her landing and does not land as he or she wanted to

Boogie: gathering of skydivers, usually more for fun than competition

Chicken soup: when a move or routine does not go as planned

Dialed in: to be synchronized with your teammate or your equipment

Drop zone, or DZ: a skydiving facility

Punch a cloud: when a skydiver falls through a cloud

Skygod: someone who is an expert skydiver; the term is also used to tease a skydiver with a big ego

The surf: a skyboard

Whuffo: a nickname given to non-jumpers

CHAPTER FOUR

GETTING AIRBORNE

While falling to Earth, divers are able to move their bodies in many directions, angles, positions, and speeds. They can fly to the left or the right, forward or backward, and right-side up or upside-down.

The major forces that affect free fall are gravity and relative wind (also known as air resistance). Gravity is the force that pulls divers toward Earth. Relative wind is the force of the wind that divers feel against their bodies as they fall. As the divers change positions, the force of wind against their bodies will increase or decrease. This happens because more or less of the divers' bodies are being exposed to the wind pushing against them. Skysurfers and freestyle skydivers must learn to balance their bodies in different positions

With hard work and practice, skysurfers learn to do many different tricks.

Some skysurfers wear webbed gloves to catch more air as they fall.

against the relative wind. By changing their body positions, these alternative flyers can perform controlled spins, rolls, and turns. When divers lose their balance against the relative wind, they can spin out of control.

Freestylers learn to perform controlled moves through practice. Even more practice is needed when a skydiver uses a skyboard. A skysurfer must learn how to balance against the relative wind with the skyboard. The skysurfer positions, angles, and moves the skyboard against the relative wind to produce different moves and effects.

X-FACTOR

There is no "sudden-drop" feeling during free fall. A sudden-drop feeling is the feeling you may have in your stomach while riding a roller coaster.

SKYDIVING TRAINING

In order to become a skysurfer, you must first master skydiving. More than 300,000 people skydive for the first time each year. While some do it only for a once-in-a-life time thrill, others do it to become skydivers or alternative flyers. There are about 250 skydiving centers across the United States. You can find out about local skydiving centers by using the United States Parachute Association's Group Member Listings (see page 44), or by looking in your phone book. The cost of attending a skydiving program is different for each center or school.

Many programs offer training or classes on alternative flying. Many centers have a minimum age

Many people choose to tandem jump on their first skydive because it takes the least amount of training.

requirement of sixteen years old for skydiving activities. The centers may also have guidelines about when a diver is skilled enough to start alternative flying.

FIRST FALLS

Most skydiving programs offer newcomers a choice of different types of jumps for their first skydive. Many drop zones offer three different options. These options are accelerated free fall (AFF), static line, and tandem. During an AFF jump, the student jumps with two instructors. The instructors hold on to the student during the exit from the plane and the free fall. They let go of the diver once his or her parachute has opened.

During a static line jump, the diver's parachute is attached to the plane with a nylon rope. The rope opens the student's parachute right after the student exits the plane. A free fall of a static line jump lasts only for about 2 seconds. By then, the parachute is fully open. In static line jumping, the student jumps from 3,500 feet (1,067 m).

During a tandem jump, the harnesses of the student and instructor are attached. The student and the instructor exit the plane, free-fall, and land together. They share one parachute system, which is operated by the instructor.

FIRST, YOU'RE GROUNDED

Before skydiving, you have to take some ground lessons. Depending on the type of jump the student chooses, the ground lessons can last from 30 minutes up to several hours. The shortest lessons are given to students jumping tandem. This is because the

The skills that are learned in skydiving school are also used when skysurfing.

instructor does most of the work in a tandem jump. All skydiving students are taught about free-falling, skydiving guidelines, and skydiving equipment. They learn when to open their parachute and how to control the canopy. They are also taught how to exit a plane and about emergency procedures. Schools usually supply the skydiving equipment.

Some skydiving schools use wind tunnels to train their students. The wind tunnel is an artificial free fall environment. It allows you to experience a free fall without being thousands of feet from Earth. Many professional skydivers use wind tunnels to train.

Ground training teaches students valuable lessons about the free fall environment. However, the best way to experience free fall is to get up in a plane and skydive. After several jumps, a skydiver learns how to control his or her body while free-falling.

LICENSE TO FLY

After their first jump, many skydivers start training to get their skydiving license. To get a license, a skydiver must demonstrate a variety of skills. He or she must be able to pack the main parachute, perform basic moves during free fall, complete at least twenty free falls, operate a parachute successfully, pass a written exam, and more. Getting a license means that the skydiver can jump without an instructor. One big benefit to getting a license is that a licensed skydiver only pays about $20 for each jump. An unlicensed skydiver can pay up to $200 for each jump.

LET'S GO SURFING NOW

The amount of time that it takes a skydiver to be ready to skysurf is different for each person.

Some divers begin to practice skysurfing after their fiftieth jump. Others don't start until after their five hundredth jump.

PRACTICE TIME

Skysurfing is a very difficult sport to learn. There are only 40 to 60 seconds of training time in the average free fall. Top-rated teams make about five hundred training jumps a year, or up to ten skydives a day during training season. A lot of time, work, and expense go into learning alternative flying.

WHAT IT TAKES

There are several skysurfing schools in the United States. These schools have their own requirements for beginning skysurfers. For example, the Perris Valley Skysurfing School requires that their students have a minimum of one hundred jumps before attending. Students must be able to change direction smoothly. They must also be able to remain in control during free fall before skysurfing.

Beginning skysurfers are trained with small skyboards. As they gain experience, they use larger boards. Larger skyboards are harder to control during free fall.

Skysurfers need special training. They must learn how to exit a plane with a skyboard attached to their feet. They will also learn to land differently because of the skyboard. Before landing, the foot bindings have to be released. Skysurfers learn to keep their feet in the unbound bindings until the last seconds of the dive.

WORTH THE WAIT

If you aren't old enough to start skydiving, you can start preparing now by getting physically fit. Also, being able to do splits, back bends, and other moves will help you greatly if you decide to take to the air. With time and patience, you too will learn why skysurfing is one of the most exciting sports on the planet.

New Words

alternative flying the general term used for sky sports, such as skysurfing and freestyle

altimeter a device that measures the distance between the skydiver and the ground

altitude the height of something above the ground

automatic activation device (AAD) a device that automatically opens the parachute when a preset altitude has been passed at high speeds

canopy the part of the parachute that catches or resists air

free fall the part of skydiving before the parachute opens

freestyle a team sport in which a skydiver performs a series of acrobatic moves during free fall

parachute the device used to slow the fall of a skydiver

relative wind the air resistance or force that a skydiver feels during free fall

rig the main parachute, reserve parachute, container, harness, and AAD

skyboard the flat board used to skysurf

skydiving the sport of jumping from an aircraft and falling freely before opening a parachute

skysurfing a team sport in which skydivers perform acrobatic moves on a skyboard during their fall

FOR FURTHER READING

Craighead, Tom. *Skydivers: Flying with Their Pants on Fire*. Lubbock, TX: Crunk Publishing, 1999.

George, Charles, and Linda George. *Team Skydiving*. Mankato, MN: Capstone Press, 1998.

Meeks, Christopher. *Skydiving*. Mankato, MN: Capstone Press, 1994.

Ryan, Pat. *Sky Surfing*. Mankato, MN: Capstone Press, 1998.

RESOURCES

Organizations

Perris Skysurfing School at Perris Valley Skydiving
P.O. Box 1823
2091 Goetz Road
Perris, CA 92570
(909) 657-3904 ext. 147
E-mail: teamfirestarter@email.com
www.teamfirestarter.com

Skydive Space Center
476 North Williams Avenue
Titusville, FL 32796
1-800-823-0016 or (321) 267-0016
Fax (321) 267-1311
E-mail: skyspace@gate.net
www.skydivespacecenter.com

RESOURCES

Skydive University
400 West Airport Drive
Sebastian, FL 32958
1-800-891-JUMP or (561) 581-0100
Fax: (561) 581-0101
www.skydiveu.com

United States Parachute Association (USPA)
1440 Duke Street
Alexandria, VA 22314
(703) 836-3495
Fax: (703) 836-2843
www.uspa.org

RESOURCES

Web Sites

Dropzone.com
www.dropzone.com
This Web site has information on drop zones around the world and many articles on sky sports.

Joe Jennings
www.joejennings.com
Read articles and see amazing pictures of Joe Jennings's work on this Web site.

Skydive World
www.skydiveworld.com
See awesome photographs, read up on your favorite sky sports, and send a greeting card to a friend on this Web site.

RESOURCES

Sport Parachutist's Safety Journal

www.MakeItHappen.com/spsj/index.html
This Web site has lots of great safety information; from protecting your altimeter to avoiding mid-air collisions with other skydivers.

The World Air Sports Federation

www.fai.org
This Web site has lots of information about air sports around the world.

INDEX

INDEX

About the Author
Holly Cefrey is a freelance writer and researcher. She is a member of the Authors Guild and the Society of Children's Book Writers and Illustrators.